LOVE IN FORMALDEHYDE
DATING ADVENTURES OF A HOLLYWOOD LASH ARTIST

SANDI SCHROEDER
WITH CHANCE G. TOMLIN

Copyright © 2017 by Sandi Schroeder, Inc.

All rights reserved. This book or any portion thereof may not be reproduced or used in any manner whatsoever without the express written permission of the publisher except for the use of brief quotations in a book review. All names have been changed for privacy reasons.

Book cover design: authentik creative, inc.

Book editing: The Artful Editor

Sesame Publishing
LA, Calif.

Printed in the United States of America

For

my clients

Table of Contents

The Business of Beauty 1

Love in Formaldehyde 7

Bumbling Brad 13

The Survival of Mrs. Robinson … Italian Style 23

Googling Gavin 33

The Pendulum Man 43

Man on Fire 51

Cheesy Charlie 63

The Hungry Hobo 73

Sociopath in the Sauna 85

The Groupon Gigolo 97

Portland Pete 107

Dating Detox 121

Acknowledgments 125

The Business of Beauty

"Who have you been dating?"

This was the question every client asked, once they settled down on the massage table, eyes closed, waiting for their biweekly refill of eyelash extensions. The person they were talking to was me.

That's what I do: make women feel good about themselves through lash extensions.

And before you laugh, consider that it's a $40 billion a year industry. And I live in Los Angeles, right in the heart of Eyelash City.

But it's not just a feel-good industry. It's also a social industry. And a therapeutic industry. My studio is a place where women come and share their stories with me. And I tell them mine too.

In fact, that's how this book was born.

My clients are always asking about my dating life. And I'm always telling them stories about the producer ex-boyfriend who blew me off on my birthday because he said he was doing night shoots. Which was fine (sort of), until I found out on Facebook he took someone else out for my birthday. Sorry I missed the party.

Then there was the story about another guy I dated ten years ago. To this day, he still uses my email to send me unsolicited requests for a loan, tax relief, or golf subscriptions. I explained to him that, No, I do not want his free Titleist travel bag with my two-year subscription. But thank you.

I told them about the son of a prominent European family who I found out a little too late is into dominatrixes who wear spandex and dildos—otherwise known as "gummy puppets." Thanks to social media, you can find out a lot if you do your research. Some of it you can never erase from your brain.

I told them about the time I went on a Tinder date with a guy with a pretty aggressive foot fetish. I thought I was just getting a foot massage but then felt my tootsies in his mouth. I never realized my dating life would lead my toes into a tug of war with a stranger's tongue.

Thanks to the world of online dating I've told my clients about the abyss of men I've found myself in. Men who call themselves Alien Candy, Slim Pipe, Honky Tonk Man, the Italian Stallion, or even Suckme.

I told them about the time I met a prospective mate on Plenty of Fish who asked me, "What the fuck our society is coming to if I'm on this site?" I had no answer for him.

And the guy who said that I "must give men boners that could drill tunnels through mountain ranges … but I mean that in a classy, substantial way of course."

From the very beginning in my career of doing eyelashes in my one-bedroom apartment, where a stoner neighbor called the cops on me for running a business out of my home, to my stint at Tracey Ross, an upscale clothing boutique, where my client base expanded to include celebrities, and now to my small private studio in West Hollywood— these were the types of stories clients continued to query me about.

We would discuss their situations as well as mine, and generally come to some conclusions (namely men are crazier than women). Most of the time we would just laugh at the ridiculousness of the dating world. But I did begin to notice a deeper thread running throughout all of our conversations. That thread was love. Every person who came in for a lash session was looking for it or facing the challenges it brought. Love was the core subject we all wanted to talk about. We were all searching for it, whether it came from a date, a marriage, a divorce, a baby, or another marriage.

My studio is the ultimate "Love Safe Space." Women lay out their stories before me and I lay out mine before them. As we shared our misadventures, the feedback I got from my clients was relief that they were not alone. We were in this together.

We're all braving the digital high seas of the dating world. We're all enduring the challenges of finding genuine communication with another. We're all wondering if once we find true love, get married, and have children, whether our kids will be able to find lasting partnerships. I listen to these stories and relate all too well because I'm out there adrift in this quest for love, too. I'm wearing a life jacket and holding a sign with big bright orange letters that says:

CAN WE TALK WITHOUT YOU SENDING ME A PICTURE OF YOUR DICK?

OR TALK ABOUT HOW GREAT YOUR ASS IS? IF SO, CALL ME.

Love in Formaldehyde

Some days I think love is toxic. It's formaldehyde.

Formaldehyde, like dating or love, is a naturally occurring organic compound. It exists as a liquid and it can actually be used to preserve things to make them last longer.

However, with just one little change, one glitch in the system, that liquid turns to gas, making it deadly to anyone who inhales it. Uh, hello? Doesn't that sound a little bit like dating?

Once you add that glitch, love turns from a liquid you know you have to be careful around into a poisonous gas you have no control over. Clearly, we are not a unique species. And the Internet preys on us, invites us to come out and play—at our own risk.

This book is a compilation of stories about my exploration into an array of curious species in the jungle of "forty-four, single, and childless." And it's also about trying to figure out whether anyone knows the rules of how to date right now. Are there rules? What's appropriate? What's the proper protocol? What's the right number of emojis to send along with your Snapchat selfies to show you are a serious person looking for love and hope to attract a like-minded creature?

It's about wondering if it's finally time to step out of the formaldehyde of the dating world and look for a different kind of love. Yes, you guessed it, it's about wondering if it's time to just say fuck it and go out and buy sperm.

And it's a story about what happens when you finally let go of what you think love should be … and find out what it really is.

*****

The check-ins, the proving where you vacation, it is just a different world. Just a few years ago, we didn't have all this social media. I have to say that for me, I admire those people who don't have a Facebook page. I think there are some good things about it, but it brings out the worst in people as well.

Bumbling Brad

"You give good phone, you know that?" His voice was warm and whispery, like it was coated with molasses and whiskey.

"Yeah, well, I'm not like the rest of the girls."

"Oh, yeah? Well, you need to prove it."

"I will. With a strap on."

"Okay. Bye."

Click.

Did this guy think I was being serious? I was perplexed. I thought he could tell I was joking. But now the only thing that was clear was that he had a serious case of anal anxiety.

Prior to this, our Tinder correspondence had been a lot of fun. From the pictures he had posted—photos of him reading a script in a suit or him hanging out with actors I'd never seen before—I had a feeling he was "in the biz."

"So, are you an agent or something?" I'd asked during our first conversation a few weeks earlier. Or, as I like to call it, "Pre strap on."

He gave me a quick and terse "Yeah." He sounded defensive, as if I'd asked him if he owned a machine gun. If you're in Hollywood and posting pics like that, what the heck else would you be? A lawyer with a theater habit? A screenwriter moonlighting as a car salesman? An usher at a movie theater? Once his profession was established, and he realized I wasn't judging him for his job representing writers at a small, albeit well-respected, talent agency, our correspondence had been witty and playful and we would talk on the phone for hours. He had a cool manner about him, similar to that of a young Karl Lagerfeld. He was sharp and seemed to get my sense of humor. After a week of great conversation, he broached the topic: "Do you want to meet up sometime next weekend?"

"I can do Sunday," I said.

"Oh, okay! Sunday. So I get the bottom of the barrel?" he said.

I was surprised. It wasn't really what I was expecting from a thirty-eight-year-old man with a good gig at an agency. Maybe, he wasn't at CAA, UTA, or WME, but still … I didn't expect him to be wearing his insecurity on his sleeve quite so soon.

But I could look past it. After all, LA breeds insecurity. In fact, it may be the city's greatest natural resource. We made a plan for Sunday dinner and moved on from there. Over the next few days, our conversations were lively and inspiring. He shared stories about his life, which were similar to mine. This, I thought, was going extremely well.

Until that fateful night when I was on my way to dinner with a girlfriend. I called him up while I was driving over to her house in Los Feliz, and we were having one of our usual dry-humor conversations. That's when the deadly "strap on" comment came tumbling out.

Goodbye, Brad. Hello, Silence! The silence started after a few days, then stretched into weeks and months … until six months later, when I was on a different dating app, Bumble. It was similar to Tinder, but everyone kept telling me that Bumble was for the more serious dater, so I figured, why not? I was a serious dater, wasn't I? Well, except when it came to making inappropriate strap-on jokes.

What was this Bumble all about? When I first heard about it, I knew I was supposed to be conjuring images of bees to pollen, but I couldn't help but think about actual bumbling. As in me, careening around, acting lost and confused in my quest for love. Would I be just another drone thrown spastically into the "location hive" with all the other drones? Floundering around, lost in search of the mysterious honey of romance?

I had only been on Bumble two days when I matched with none other than Brad, the agent. Really? Did I want to get back into Brad-ville? I decided, why not? This could be a chance to redeem myself from the dreaded strap-on snafu. Happily, Brad and I reconnected with the same great easygoing conversation. He never referenced my aforementioned faux pas. Maybe he had repressed the memory.

He wanted to meet me at a place on Third Street called Simple Things. I suggested a Thursday lunch to avoid any kind of "bottom of the barrel" feelings on his part. I found parking easily and walked inside. Simple Things is a quaint, cozy place known for salads and mini key lime pies. I immediately felt at ease and sat down at a corner table to wait for him. Next to me there was a woman with a fat, red Buddha tattooed on her leg. She was having a really loud conversation on her phone about being lactose intolerant. Next to her was a guy with a flannel shirt sipping an iced cappuccino and reading Ayn Rand.

I called my friend, Jessica, and asked her if any of the predictions had come true from the psychic reading she had had last week. It seemed like the right thing to do in this particular environment.

Finally, Brad entered the restaurant. He was tall and his CrossFit build tightly filled out his suit. He had beautiful, fine features and plump lips. He gave me a shaky handshake and really, really intense eye contact as I ended my phone call. It was actually a little scary. He had this controlling, *Silence of the Lambs* kind of energy.

"Who were you talking to?" he asked, his eyes probing mine.

"Oh, just talking with a friend of mine," I said. He sat down while maintaining that psychotic, laser-beam gaze.

"It's not Sunday, you know? Let's just chill out a little bit here," I said, smiling, trying to break the tension. He relaxed a little bit and his gaze dropped from laser beam to bright flashlight, but he still had a general shakiness about him. I guess maybe he was nervous? I could totally understand it; dating is a completely vulnerable and terrifying thing. But there was something about his energy that was making my energy feel like it wanted to run for its life.

In order to stop thinking about his shaking hands and probing eyeballs, I focused on a skin tag above his right eyelid. Was that something that he could get fixed, but chose not to? I wondered if it would be out of place for me to recommend a dermatologist to him. I quickly derailed my instinct to give him skin care advice and focused instead on his shirt and suit. I was guessing the shirt was Gucci, but the suit looked like it was from was Loehmann's. Not that there's anything wrong with Loehmann's, I chided myself. But it was clear that I was focusing on negative things because poor Brad was not the guy for me. I should have realized that six months ago, when I wondered if he was a lawyer with a theater habit.

After we ordered lunch, we finally got into a flow of easy conversation. We discussed European travel and movies and shared a love of both. But then he began doing this weird thing where he would reach out across the table and grab my hand and just hold it and say, "Wow," followed by an intense stare after he delivered the word WOW. Hand grabbing? Darkly possessive eye contact? Mooney-eyed declaration of "Wow"? I couldn't wait for this date to be over.

Our lunch finally came to an end, and we walked out to his car. I turned and gave him a hug. Then I let go and he stared at me. "Really? That's it? You know how I feel about you."

I was totally baffled. "Uhhh …"

He cut me off. "You're a prude!" he announced.

Really? Me? The girl who had a job doing phone sex in college? Who's been an innocent bystander at swingers' parties as a caterer? Who's been privy to more than one threesome, for crying out loud! My slut pride was wounded.

But I figured explaining all my sexual forays to him was not the best exit strategy. So I just nodded and said, "Me, a prude? You have no idea! See ya around!" I walked away and got into my car.

Once I made sure he had driven away and was no longer in sight, I sat in my car for a minute thinking about why he would think that I would make out with him at two in the afternoon after a first lunch date.

Needless to say, twenty-five minutes later, I received a text from Brad: "You have a nice little figure on your frame. I would not mind exploring it in greater detail."

Are you freaking kidding me?!

I responded with a simple, "*Thanks.*"

He texted back: "You are welcome. That was a nice lunch."

I send him a neutral "kiss" emoticon wishing there was a "kiss my ass" emoticon instead.

Later, that night, I felt a few pings of pity for poor Brad. Who taught him to act like this?

But thanks to my time with Brad, I learned that sometimes it's better not to get to know a guy too much over the phone. As sparkling as that repartee can be, it's likely going to create an image of a person that doesn't exist. And then you end up forced to eat a salad and a mini key lime pie for an hour and a half with a guy with a skin tag on his eyelid.

And if a guy can't take a strap-on joke, then chances are *he's* the prude.

*****

Potential Mate: So have you dated younger?

Me: Yes, of course.

Potential Mate: I'm 26 …

Me: Umm … U are?

Potential Mate: I generally date older women.

Me: Oh. Why?

Potential Mate: Confidence, maturity, better chemistry and higher sex drive … to name a few

Me: Good point

The Survival of Mrs. Robinson ... Italian Style

Thanks to a great girlfriend, I'd been invited to attend a beauty show in Bologna, Italy. I had high hopes that the Italian component would be a good ego boost. Mine needed it, since I hadn't gone on a date in seven months. I landed in Bologna at 8:00 am, and after strolling through the city, eating Nutella gelato, and buying a pair of shoes, I sat in my hotel room jetlagged and wide-awake at 3:00 am. I was blessed to be reminded of my loneliness as my girlfriend and her husband had exuberant sex in the room next door.

I had no choice. I had to join Tinder in Italy. And wow, were people right about Italian men!

Within seven minutes, I had fifteen men greeting me with messages of, "Ciao Bella, Ciao, Bellisima!" It felt great! But there was one Tinder guy in particular who was very persistent throughout my short stay. He didn't seem to be a weirdo and he certainly wasn't unattractive. His name was Carlo and he was a blonde, green-eyed, six-foot Italian Adonis who was totally, I kind of want to say, *stalking* me. He gave me five good reasons why we should meet:

1. U r American.

2. U r blonde.

3. When will I ever meet a Californian blonde? (Little did he know that this Californian blonde was really from New York.)

4. I would like to show you around Bologna.

5. I need to practice my English.

Okay, the last reason was not so sexy, but I was sold nonetheless. As a woman in her forties, I figured this was probably the hottest, most interested man I'd met on Tinder in a while. At least he wasn't an unemployed actor of dubious

25

sexual orientation. If he wanted to learn about grammar and conjugation, who was I to stand in his way?

But scheduling proved to be difficult. I had absolutely no real free time on this trip because the beauty show was from 9:00 am to 7:00 pm every day, and so I had to keep canceling our meet-ups. Then, my friend and her husband announced they were going to Rome and the place we were staying was no longer available. Could I get a hotel room?

Blessedly, another Tinder message from Carlo the Italian popped up: "Can you meet tonight? I can cook you dinner at my apartment? I am desperate to see you."

It was like the pope himself was ordaining a solution. This was a way to be spontaneous and economically savvy.

So, on my last night in Bologna, I arrived at Via degli Scalini 8, lugging my two, 13x10 suitcases, and a carry-on up his staircase.

I climbed the few short steps to his door and stood there a moment before ringing the buzzer. Is this really what I wanted to be doing? Going on a first date with a complete stranger and then having to stay the night with him? His green eyes, his gorgeous smile, and sweet messages of romance flashed in my head. So I took a deep breath and rang the buzzer. I heard a quick, nervous voice through the speaker, "Un momento!"

He sounded more nervous than I was. *How cute is that?* After about three minutes and the sound of footsteps descending what must have been at least four flights of stairs, the door opened and Carlo, the Italian Adonis, appeared.

He was gorgeous, but he seemed much younger than I remembered him from his profile, like there was no way he was much over twenty-one. His head was down and he was much meeker than his hard-sell Tinder persona indicated. I looked down at my suitcases. *How was I going to find a hotel while lugging all my bags and without speaking a word of Italian?* Since my flight was at 6:00 am, I knew I would have to endure whatever may come.

"Hi Carlo," I said with a big smile. "Nice to meet you!"

Without blinking or even really speaking, he hauled my two suitcases up four flights of stairs. Once he led me inside his one-bedroom apartment, he began asking questions: "So, how do you like it here? How was the beauty show?"

His manner was extremely anxious. I was almost old enough to be his mother. As I looked around, I started to detect a definite college vibe to the apartment. There was a worn brown leather couch, a bare-bones wooden table, a thirteen-inch television, and random flea market art on the walls. There was also the fact that he looked young enough to possibly be my child.

He asked me if I wanted some wine and then he informed me that my choices for dinner would be either chicken or beef. This was certainly starting out better than most dates that I'd experienced back in LA, where men took you out for snacks or fast food. Being with Carlo was like flying business class.

I decided on the chicken, and he brought me a glass of red wine before he proceeded to lay the chicken breast out on the kitchen table and begin pounding it. I mean really pounding it. He was whacking it with the side of a meat cleaver with such intensity that it rattled the bottle of wine on the counter.

"What are you doing to that poor chicken?" I asked him.

"It makes the meat more tender!" he said with a shy, little smile.

The few times guys in LA had made me dinner, they presented me with portions so small they were almost undetectable to the naked eye. Now, here was a twenty-two-year-old hunk who was concerned about the consistency of the meat. I had to say I felt like I was in good hands.

He served me a lovely meal and he practiced his English. He wanted to know if everyone in California drove a Prius. He wanted to know why I wasn't more tan and if my friends were celebrities. As I answered his queries, he rolled a cigarette for me.

His "chicken" was indeed tender. Naturally. *It was only twenty-two.*

Dinner ended and we sat on the couch trying our best to keep up the conversation through broken English, which proved somewhat challenging. Finally, we both just fell silent. A minute passed, then another. It seemed to last forever. He gave me a puzzled look before finally breaking the silence with a question, "That's it?"

Okay, this made me a little nervous. It was midnight in a town where I didn't know anyone. I might as well have been on Mars. And did I mention that I had no Euros left because I didn't want to exchange any more money? For the record, I was being frugal, not cheap. But the results were the same. I was stuck.

"What do you mean, 'that's it?'" I said.

"Tinder!" he said stumbling with his reply. "It's about sex, yes? But you sit there and do nothing."

"Oh, okay … so what do you want?" I said. He just sat there silent like a kid who was being punished by his teacher. Tipsy on wine and hand-rolled cigarettes, I thought, *fuck it*. If Mrs. Robinson is what he wants, Mrs. Robinson is what he'll get.

I grabbed his hand and led him to his bedroom. When I say bedroom, I mean a spare, empty room with two single beds in it. The beds were exactly the same type of box spring-free mattress you sleep on at camp.

I threw him down on one of the beds and heard that springy sound as he fell onto the mattress. He had a look like he was struck by lightning. But, hey, he wanted Tinder and I decided I was going to give him some flame.

And how was the sex? Well, he tried. But all I could concentrate on while we were doing it was the sound of those squeaky springs on the bed and how they needed to be oiled up or something. Then I started to drift off thinking about how I may have to force his hand at fetching me a cab in the morning and paying for it since I was in no mood to exchange any more Euros. I just wanted to be on my flight to LA nestled comfortably on the plane flying back to the safety of my home.

The time passed slowly, and as I lay there listening to random Italians yelling downstairs along with the random honks of cars, I felt a hand approach my leg and the caressing started. *Here we go again.*

Well, I'm not even going to explain or give too much description to this act other than the fact that it happened. I did what I had to do and then the alarm went off at 4:00 am, alerting me that it was time to *ciao*. I got quickly dressed, thanked him, and proceeded to make it down all four flights of stairs. He grabbed my luggage, hailed a cab, spoke to the driver in Italian, and handed him some money. *YAY, no problem there.*

We did a kiss-type of thing cheek to cheek and I was on my way. I have to say, there was no telling where I was being taken at that time of morning. I guess you just have to trust sometimes, and as Oprah says: *There are no mistakes.*

I made it to the Bologna airport, muddled through ticketing and security, and then planted myself in my seat for the thirteen-hour flight. As I nestled back into my seat, I reflected on Carlo. Despite his young age, he had more manners than any LA man I'd ever dated.

It's been two years now, and I still continue to receive messages from the Italian Adonis checking in and telling me how he would love to come visit me in LA. More recently though, the messages have become Snapchat messages. They're appreciated ... for now.

*****

I'm not the kind of girl who puts lipstick on every twenty minutes. I don't take an hour to get ready. Give me ten minutes and I'm done. All in all, I'm pretty low-maintenance. My one vice would be hair extensions. I hate going through airport security because every time they have to pull me aside and pat down my head, I want to scream: Yes, my hair is fake, okay?!? Do you have to make me admit it in front of all of LAX?

Googling Gavin

Sometimes we connect with people on social media that we already know or used to know. Gavin is one of those people. Gavin was a classmate of mine when we went to boarding school in our early teens. I felt a comfortability factor there. It's cool when you can use social media to reconnect with people from different stages in your life, so I was interested when Gavin reached out to me on Facebook. He thought it would be a great idea if we could meet up and I agreed. *Why not?*

I always remembered Gavin as being smart, cute, and funny. He used to wear bow ties with shined shoes and always made jokes, which usually made everyone either blush or be uncomfortable. In all of the correspondence leading up to our date, Gavin was surprisingly flirtatious. I could sense that his sexual humor was still brewing under the surface. The day before our date, he confirmed and said how excited he was to see me.

We met at a bookstore on Ventura Boulevard. I was hanging out in the autobiography section when he walked in, skimming through Holly Madison's autobiography, *Down the Rabbit Hole*, a book about her life at the Playboy Mansion (which is, by the way, a fascinating read). Gavin was wearing a black, straw fedora hat and freshly shined shoes. He looked the same except that his bright red *MAD Magazine* hair was shaved off, his stomach had filled out, and he had an added air of distinction with his black Tom Ford frames.

"Well, wow!" he said, looking me up and down like a wolf in one of those old cartoons.

From the bookstore we went to have a "snack." Being that we had attended boarding school together, I'd hoped he'd be well versed in the ways of etiquette, but he walked in front of me and didn't hold any doors open. When it was time to order food, he put in his order first. I excused myself to go to the bathroom, and when I returned he was smiling and holding up something that looked like it belonged on my head. One of my extensions had fallen out onto my chair. "Is this yours?" he asked.

"Yes," I said, mortified, stashing it into my purse.

As embarrassing as it was, the hair situation served to break the ice. We ended up having a great time and soon we started to see each other at least four times a week. Before I knew it, we were in a relationship. We would go to Venice and walk the boardwalk, take in *Sixteen Candles* or *Ferris Bueller's Day Off* at the Hollywood Forever Cemetery, or watch his son's baseball practice (yes, he had a son). We even went on the TMZ bus one day, pretending we were tourists. Soon, any poor manners he had were overlooked because I was having such a good time. Little did I know at the time that a massive tropical storm was brewing. A storm called "Googling Gavin."

It all started with my plan to go to Hawaii for my birthday. Unfortunately, Gavin couldn't exactly afford the trip, so I offered to pay his way. I didn't mind because I knew we'd have a great time. That was until he met Dorsa.

Dorsa was one of my best friends, and I thought she and Gavin could maybe collaborate on a business project together, so a few days before our trip I set up a meeting for the three of us to meet at the Palihouse, a restaurant at a hotel in West Hollywood.

Dorsa and I had drinks while he nursed a coffee. We moved from drinks into dinner (my treat) and then decided we should continue the party elsewhere because WE WERE ALL HAVING SUCH A GOOD TIME. Big mistake.

Things had already started to get a little weird at the restaurant when Gavin began subjecting us to stories about himself and his two friends, Leo and Toby. Evidently, ten years ago, the three of them considered themselves to be the "pussy posse" of young Hollywood. The name drop wasn't lost on me.

As we were in the lounge figuring out where to go next, Dorsa said, "If we're going out, maybe I should put my face on."

Gavin then looks at her and says, "If I had your face on my …"

What?!? Did he think he was still in the pussy posse?

I stopped him right there with a firm slap across his face. Everyone went totally silent. Gavin asked me to step outside with him. Feeling horribly guilty, I did. That was until he proceeded to deny saying what we all heard him say. But now all I'm thinking about was:

A. This guy is a dick.

B. I just slapped him in a public place.

C. I'm about to go on a trip to Hawaii with this mofo.

As you can imagine, it was all downhill from there. Starting from that evening, to him sleeping on the couch, to the five-hour plane ride, everything felt strained, like an aching calf muscle that was finally starting to tear in the twenty-fifth mile of a marathon. But I persevered, hoping that once we landed on the beautiful sands of Oahu, maybe the energy would change.

We got to The Royal Hawaiian, the pinkest, oldest hotel in Oahu, a stone's throw from the lullaby surf of Waikiki Beach. That energy change I was hoping for? Forget about it. I was filled with a sense of dread and horror even with the tropical breezes that seemed to promise the most romantic vacay ever. But there was no romance; it felt like we were a couple that had been separated and had to keep our relationship together just for the sake of the kids. From the outside, we looked like a perfect couple wearing our flower leis, decked out in our Hawaiian-inspired outfits. We frolicked in the warm waters, went to a luau, ate great food, and hiked Diamond Head, where he proceeded to take selfies to send to "friends back in LA."

Then, on our next to last night, he left his cell phone by the edge of the hot tub while he left to go to the gift shop. I was sitting there, de-stressing, when a text from "Sara" popped up on his phone. I picked it up and casually scrolled through his texts.

Text after text it got worse. Here he was confirming his undying love for her, saying how he wished he was with her and how he didn't love me; and once he got some money together, he could be with her. All of this romance was sent to her with the occasional scenic selfie thrown in for good measure. He was texting another woman right under my nose while having me pay for literally everything he possibly could. What kind of person with any conscience would ever continue having someone pay for everything while proclaiming their love to someone else? I felt like the pink walls of The Royal Hawaiian were closing in around me and I wished I could have just charged out to the ocean and swum back home.

After reading those texts, however, I knew I had to remain composed. I put his phone back at the hot tub's edge, took a long sip from my Mai Tai, and waited for him to return, feeling like I had fire running through my veins. I had so many mixed emotions. I was mad at myself, at him, at society, at Hawaii. Which is horrible because it's one of the most beautiful places on the planet, and now it felt tarnished because of this experience, like someone pouring sulfuric acid on a Fabergé egg. He returned in a chipper mood.

Instead of attacking him, I decided to show him nothing. I just wanted to get through this experience with some class and dignity. I acted totally normal for the rest of the trip and while it was hard, I did it. Sometimes you have to choose your battles because otherwise you wind up blowing yourself up in so many ways it's hard to put the pieces back together.

The plane trip back was agonizing. He tried to act all cuddly when we boarded and then fell asleep on me for the rest of the flight. As he slept peacefully next to me, I wanted to stab him with one of my eyelash tools. But I kept my cool. I ordered a gin and tonic and stared out the window. There were fantastic, sun-tipped clouds in the distance forming jagged mountains in midair. The ocean below seemed frozen in time but yet completely alive. It was a churning, primordial birthplace of life itself. Was there love at the bottom of the ocean? Or was it all darkness, uncertainty, and survival?

Looking out at my surroundings jolted me with a feeling that I was a part of something bigger than myself. I felt momentarily connected to the descendants of those original ancient fish from millions of years ago, who through years of struggle had slowly, painfully crawled their way onto shore, adapting to new forms, finding new ways of being alive. Doesn't love have something to do with this? Does this search for love at least mimic that struggle?

Our plane finally landed and I drove him back to his place. The ride was mostly silent. As he got out of the car, I told him to take care. I meant it. I drove home up the windy hills to Laurel Canyon. I realized that I do believe there's love at the bottom of the ocean and in the world in general. I just hadn't found mine yet.

I got home, fell into bed, switched off the light, and slept better than I had in a whole month. A phone next to a hot tub in a pink hotel had taught me that even though my dreams of true love with my former boarding school classmate weren't meant to be, they weren't impossible with someone else.

*****

A man asks me out on Facebook. I decline.

He asks again.

I can't.

I see a notice on Facebook that he passed away three months later.

Argh, now I feel bad ... and sad.

The Pendulum Man

The actual definition of tinder is a dry, flammable material such as wood or paper, used for lighting a fire. It sounds useful, right? However, the definition of Tinder, the dating app, is probably best defined by a question proposed by Urban Dictionary enthusiast Sweet Dick Tony, who ladled out this heavy wisdom from Internet mountain:

"How can I creep on girls on my phone?"

"Tinder."

Useful? Maybe. *Maybe not.*

But there I was on Tinder. Looking for what? *Kindling? Am I trying to build a fire?* And if so, am I just trying to get warm or do I want to burn something down? It's really hard to tell anymore. But then it happened: the match.

Randy was an acupuncturist, forty-one, tall, with two offices and a black belt. I can see now maybe the warning signs were already there. Perhaps not the most relaxed man on earth.

But we had some good conversations on the app about spirituality, and so we decided to meet up. We arranged for a simple, quick meeting at my place on a Tuesday afternoon. He had plans later that evening, but we both agreed it would be great if he stopped by so we could at least meet each other in person. Especially after the last lesson I learned with Brad. Besides, I'd had a long day at work, with no less than six clients back-to-back, and I didn't feel like going out somewhere.

Later that day, I was eagerly waiting for his arrival when I heard this awful screeching coming from my garage downstairs. It sounded like the hull of a ship grinding into an iceberg. Evidently, my Tinder match was trying to squeeze his car into my garage. *My garage.* A garage that really only fits one car and that one car was already parked there. Maybe it was the confidence that his martial arts expertise gave him? I'm not exactly sure. But I couldn't help but think: *Who just presumes* they can use someone else's garage, especially when it's very clear that their car won't even fit?

The violence of his parking method made me wonder if he may have some deeper anger or frustration issues. Why had the wisdom from his more spiritual endeavors failed to give him the right tools to park his car like a normal person? Especially, when there was plenty of parking on the street.

He walked up the stairs to my front door flashing a big, toothy smile. I held the door open and attempted to give him a hug with one arm.

"Oh no, I need a two-handed hug!" he said.

I invited him in while thinking in the back of my mind I would just make this a very light and friendly "nice to finally meet you" and that would be it. No big deal. But then the situation took an unexpected turn.

"Is there a spirit in your home?" he asked as he stepped inside.

Hmm, what an odd question.

"I don't believe so," I said.

Luckily, he didn't ask me any more questions about spirits while we chatted in the kitchen, but he quickly turned the conversation to his acupuncture practice, his meditation rituals, and his gallantry as a black belt. The conversation seemed to have no end in sight, and I had a hard time getting a word in edgewise. Until he finally paused and pulled out a small crystal tied to a long chain.

"What is that?" I asked.

"Oh this?" he asked. He gently swung the crystal from side to side. "This is my pendulum," he said. "And I consult it for EVERYTHING." He raised his eyebrows and narrowed his eyes tightly on the spinning crystal.

"*Everything?*" I asked.

"Absolutely. It allows me to access the Universal Mind through the energy patterns of my subconscious vibrations."

I wanted to ask him if he had consulted his pendulum about trying to park his car in my garage earlier but decided against it.

Now, let's get one thing straight, I consider myself to be a spiritual person. I believe in the possibility of an afterlife, and I've gone to a few psychics. But a guy who carries around a pendulum to determine life's answers? This was a new one.

He walked into the living room and made himself comfortable on my couch. He held his pendulum above his left hand as he explained how it worked. "By relaxing and allowing my inner vibrations to connect to the higher etheric plane, I can link to the other side and ask spirits questions." He then took a deep breath.

"Was someone killed in this house?" he asked his pendulum. The pendulum began to sway clockwise. "AHA! I knew it!" he said. "I could feel it when I first walked in! Yes, the pendulum says."

Great, I thought. Where is this going?

"Were they killed in the living room?" No, the pendulum says. "The hallway?" The pendulum says no again. "The bedroom?"

"Please, don't ask that," I said. "I mean, really how am I supposed to get any sleep knowing someone was murdered in my bedroom?"

He squinted his eyes at me and asked, "Was the kitchen the site of the murder?" The pendulum sways and says YES. This was getting too much for me. Was I expected to casually cook myself dinner every night in a crime scene?

He was about to ask the pendulum another question when I stopped him. "I think you're going to be late for your other meeting. Probably best for you to go now."

He stood up off the couch and abruptly left, saying a terse goodbye.

An hour later I received a text from him. He asked me what I thought of him, and I never responded. Maybe he should have consulted with his pendulum? Perhaps he had, and it told him that we were definitely going to see each other again.

It's difficult to imagine being with a man who uses a crystal on a string to make life's decisions. I'm not here to judge, but I do think if you're interested in a woman, maybe don't pull out your pendulum on the first date. Just keep the thing in your pants. Then when you get to the privacy of your own home, you can pull it out and ask it all the questions you want.

*****

Me: I have to say I am really looking forward to meeting you!

Potential Mate: Yes, me too, I can't wait to kiss you. My kiss is a combination of a summer's breeze and a firm handshake.

Me: Umm, weird.

Man on Fire

When you hear the name eHarmony, you might think of bliss and happiness. You think of easygoing, no-nonsense people. That's what I thought too. I was, as usual, in for a surprise.

Jack was a fifty-two-year-old dude who totally did not look his age whatsoever. He surfed and was also a passionate music festival-goer. His yearly highlights were going to the Electric Daisy Carnival, Lightning in a Bottle, Coachella, the Redding Festival, and, of course, that most sacred of holy pilgrimages, Burning Man.

I researched more about Burning Man and "life on the playa." I learned about the phenomenon known as "playa dust"—clay dust that is finer than talcum powder. Playa dust, it's been stated, contains 100 percent RDA of everything a body needs for survival. Apparently, playa dust can restore your lost foreskin, as well as melt warts!

With these tidbits in mind, I made plans for Jack to drive from Malibu to meet me in LA for dinner. Our plans were coming together nicely—until he checked the surf conditions for Malibu the following morning. It turns out they were "rad." Our date quickly became secondary to this oceanic new development. The surf is the Bible, and I was destined to be a mistress to the surf. Now, I want to be cool and chill, but I also want to be respected. It was moments like that one that made me take a big step back from the fuzzy warmth of Jack's flames. But I was drawn to his positivity and was taken with my fantasy of making it work with someone more "mature" who could take care of me once in a while.

As the following weekend approached, he asked me to come out to spend the weekend with him in his rented Malibu track home. He mentioned it was on the same street as Cher, Mel, Streisand … you get the gist.

Jack also held the special key for the coveted "beach access," which separates the haves from the have-nots out in "The

Bu." The weather was supposed to be eighty-seven degrees, with clear skies. We had the makings of an ideal "Mature Date." I racked up my lease miles and went for it. I was eager to see what the day held romantically, and even sexually. I even brought my THC spray, which you spray directly onto your clitoris in order to achieve multiple orgasms. There was a two-month expiration date for the spray and, sadly, I hadn't found an occasion to use it with anyone yet. It was now or never.

I arrived at Jack's house, and basked in the ocean breeze and the fresh air hitting my skin. I felt my anxieties dropping like away like playa sand. Jack greeted me at the front porch, which was heavily laden with flip-flops of all sizes and colors. He greeted me with a giant soul hug and several intense soul squeezes. I fought to silence the alarm on my Cheeseball Radar, which was starting to blare.

"Howdy, babe, great to see you," he said, leading me into his house. He seemed nervous and excited at the same time. He began rambling to fill the quasi-uneasy silence, telling me about the plans he had made for us for the next forty-eight hours. I couldn't help but feel a little worried about the time commitment. But I reminded myself to get into a Malibu state of mind as he offered to show me his beach access. He instructed me to slip on a pair of flip-flops as we went down to the beach. I've never been keen to insert my toes into other peoples' footwear, but again, I tried to remind myself to be as chill and beach-like as possible.

As he gave me the tour, I was confused by the fact that he walked in front of me and spoke forward into the wind, his back towards me. After a while, I would just nod my head because it was easier than constantly shouting, "I'm sorry, what?"

We walked down the beach for a while like that, with me nodding like a bobble head because I had no idea what he was saying. Eventually, we ended up at Paradise Cove Cafe, which had a similar vibe to the Hamptons, except the people are from Orange County instead of the Upper East Side. We had some fruity drinks and a shrimp cocktail with a very spicy cocktail sauce while we watched the eclectic array of beachgoers. We stayed there for a few hours and then moseyed back along the beach, engaging in more muffled conversation. When we got back to his house, we took a nap. He threw some pillows and a blanket out on his futon, laid down on it, and motioned me to "come hither."

    I joined him. As he wrapped his arms around me and cuddled me, I started to feel ill, either from the too spicy cocktail sauce or the tight hold. I actually ended up passing out, but before I knew it, I jolted up in a state of confusion as he was waking me with wet kisses. Fortunately, that didn't cause too much of a kerfuffle because he reminded me it was time to go see an independent film by a friend of his at the Malibu Country Mart.

    As we made our way to the movie in his super surfer-friendly SUV, he began to test me on my musical knowledge. "Okay, let's play a music guessing game," he said with a coy smile.

    "Okay, I guess," I responded.

    "It's really easy, just guess the artist."

    "Gotcha."

    As he turned up the dial on the radio, I panicked, not knowing who was singing. "Uhhh …"

    To help me out, he started to sloooooowly say the name of the artist, stretching the syllables like a tape dubbed in slow motion. "BBOOOOOOOBB DIIILLLLOOONNN," he said, finishing with a big smile.

    For the next song, I decided to jump in. I could do this! I really could.

    "Bahhh …?" He hinted.

    "BOB DYLAN!" I half-shouted.

"Yep! You've got the hang of this," he said. This continued for several songs. After a full minute of him trying to slowly say, and I mean, like, slowly, in the slowest motion ever, the name "Siiiiiiiiimmmoonn and Gaarrrrrrfunkel," I felt like I might be going slightly insane. Then, it was over. Or was it? Another song came on and the slow-motion nightmare started all over again. It became obvious that my knowledge of classic rock was painfully scant.

Finally we arrived at the theater, and I was grateful to sit and not have to play the music guessing game again. He held my hand and began to baby-feed me popcorn and Ju Ju Beans. I opened my mouth obediently, but I considered biting at his hand. I just wanted to sit silently in the dark and watch the movie. Instead, I was being fed as though I were a baby pet monkey. I silently chanted Simon and Garfunkel lyrics over and over to myself in order to avoid a violent physical attack.

On the drive back to his Malibu house, playing yet another round of the music game, I thought to myself, *This is it*. I fantasized about the moment we arrived at the house, and I could get in my car and go home. But then I reminded myself that that would be rude. Here was a guy who had planned a full forty-eight-hour Mature Date for us. I had to see it through. Plus, I had to try out a round of my clitoris spray, because that expiration date was getting closer by the second. I convinced myself that if I could just focus on the multiple orgasms, maybe, I'd be okay. We actually had a lovely time. He was super affectionate, tender, and smelled amazing. This clitoris spray was good stuff!

The following morning, however, I was thrust back into the nightmare that was Jack. He awoke and began pawing at me with a dog-like vigor. He was like a mosquito drawn to the sweetest blood ever. I like affectionate men, but this was beyond.

"We are pretty much together now that we have spent all this time together …"

It felt like the walls of life caving in on me. What was he talking about?!? This was supposed to be an experiment in maturity, not an instant relationship!

I told him that I was not anyone's girlfriend. I was going to be with whomever I choose to be with. I explained that I had zero plans to ever rush into something.

He smiled lovingly at me, "Oh, babe, your blood sugar is probably low. That must be why you're feeling so upset."

"Let's grab some breakfast," he continued. "We'll hang out later with a couple of friends of mine that I know from Burning Man. They wanted to use the key to get beach access later anyways."

As soon as I heard this, I started to feel anxious. I thought I had come to Malibu to get to know this man and spend some time with him, not his friends from the Playa. I reminded myself to take a deep breath of ocean air and try to breathe through it.

He took me to Moonshadows for breakfast, where things started to improve. Sitting out on the patio overlooking the water, the smell of breakfast food, laughter … how great was this! Over eggs Benedict, he asked me if I was open to discussing a situation he had been in for over ten years.

"What do you mean?" I asked. My interest was piqued. As he reached across the table to baby feed me my food, he began to tell me about his situation, which involved an Asian woman named Marie. I wondered where this was going. He explained that he had been seeing Marie for a long time. He slept with her in between his relationships, he said, but he could never break free from deep feelings he held for her. In fact, he was in love with her. I was so confused. Why was he telling me about being in love with a woman while we were on a breakfast date?

I stared at him, "Why are you continuing to have relationships with other women if you have so many feelings for Marie?"

"Well," he said. "She's married."

"What?" I was confused.

"She's married."

So she was cheating on her husband? Does she still sleep with him? I began peppering Jack with questions. I couldn't quite tell what I was feeling, but it definitely wasn't a feeling of being respected and appreciated. Here was a guy who was truly in love with a woman he couldn't be with … so he chose to have beach time with me? I felt bad for all the other women who had been in my shoes over the past ten years. How many of us had he played the music guessing game with while he was pining for the unavailable Marie?

He explained that in the Asian culture, Chinese culture specifically, people aren't allowed to get divorced. I was dubious. That sounded like an excuse, but who was I to doubt Marie's intentions? I decided to try to suppress my agitation and go with the flow. Baggage like this was probably part and parcel to Mature Dating. So we continued the day with a little shopping and walking on the beach and hanging out.

When we got back to the house, in anticipation of his friends' arrival, Jack ordered a pizza. The pizza delivery guy showed up half an hour later, and Jack began frantically searching for money. I walked in and caught him holding a jar of change, carefully picking out quarters, dimes, and nickels. I asked him if he needed some money for the pizza, and he replied, "Nah, just need to get this guy a good tip." The delivery guy was standing in the doorway looking uncomfortable, waiting for the transaction to be over. As Jack handed the delivery guy a huge handful of change, I realized I might have reached my limit. I'd had enough Malibu Weekend Fun. After much soul-squeezing and hugging and promises for more breakfasts, I excused myself.

As I drove down the beach access road and pulled onto the Pacific Coast Highway, I breathed a sigh of relief. I rolled the windows down and took a deep inhalation of salty air. I was finally experiencing that sensation that people spend years going to Burning Man to try to capture: pure, unadulterated freedom.

*****

It's rare that a man will approach me in LA and give me a compliment. But I have found when I go to The Abbey, a hot gay bar in West Hollywood, I usually have several men approach and compliment me on how I look or give some other friendly bit of praise about my clothes or my general vibe. Straight men? Nada. This town seems so backwards sometimes.

Cheesy Charlie

Charlie was a tall, cute, sexy Aussie with an easygoing personality. I met him through OkCupid, which is yet another odd name for a website. What's really going on with this Cupid? Is Cupid telling me it's okay? How am I supposed to trust a chubby, little baby flying around on angel's wings with a bow and a handful of arrows? Some of these arrows are dipped with poison lead and half the time he's been known to be completely blindfolded. They say love is blind, right? So what's it going to be? Are you going to get hit with an arrow of Happily Ever After? Or are you going to get whacked with the thumpity-thump of heavy-duty, old-fashioned lead? All I do know is that putting your love life in the hands of a flying, blindfolded baby, running around half-cocked with a set of weapons, is definitely a sign that this could be a surefire road to heartbreak.

But OkCupid had already struck, and Charlie had left a message that actually came across as sincere and pretty adorable. I called him back, and we spoke for a decent amount of time before setting up a date. We had easy, fun, flirty chitchat, and all throughout, he kept saying, "You give good phone."

Maybe that was a vestigial skill left over from my stint as a phone sex operator in college. It's a talent that can come in handy every now and then, although I wasn't quite ready to share that with him.

Charlie and I decided to meet at The Hudson, a festive bar in West Hollywood … and things really took off from there. We ended up going to four other places that night because we were having such a great time. I told him about my recent choice to freeze my eggs, and he told me about his parents' divorce when he was eighteen. He also told me that he had back surgery just a couple of weeks ago, pulling up his shirt to show me the scar, and holding up screenshots of his x-rays on his phone. Because of his recent back surgery, we would actually have to get to know each other before having any serious intimacy. With all of these "hookup" apps where it seemed like people had become so disposable, this was a welcome change.

The rest of the night was fantastic. He was a whirlwind of flattery and compliments. He kept saying things like, "Where have you been all this time? I think we should defrost your eggs!"

He then grabbed a total stranger to take our picture together, saying that we needed a photo because we were getting married next week. He said that he wanted to see me again before I left on my upcoming trip to Arizona, where I would spend a few days in the bottom of the Grand Canyon visiting my brother. I told him that would be great, and that Tuesday would work. He said he would bring over dinner and cook. Did I like salmon? I love salmon! I was impressed. A guy who offers to come over and cook salmon, my favorite food? *Sign me up.*

Well, Tuesday arrived and so did Charlie carrying a bag from Trader Joe's tucked under his arm. It was great to see him. We made our usual fun, flirty small talk, but I became distracted when I saw what he was pulling out of the bag.

The salmon he prepared was literally the size of a baby's fist. I usually ate a portion twice that size on my own. He had brought a few other items: crackers, Havarti cheese, and the ingredients to make a salad. The salad was crafted in miniature as well, like a bonsai tree made of microgreens and herbs. I must have had a look of concern on my face, or an odd frown because he asked, "What's up? Everything okay?"

I quickly snapped out of it, shaking my head, and said, "Oh, yeah! *Totally.* Sorry, I was just remembering something I had to do." Even with the dollhouse portions, we had a nice dinner and I reminded myself that it was amusing more than anything else. Again, how nice was it that he came over and cooked for me? However, at the end of the night, and after we'd cleared the table and he was getting ready to go, he pulled out the Trader Joe's bag. "I'm going to need to take the cheese with me," he said.

"What?" I asked him.

"I'm taking the cheese back," he said as he began wrapping the tiny sliver of Havarti and putting it back in the bag with the crackers.

"Oh, sure. Whatever you want," I said. What I was really thinking was: *Who takes a sliver of cheese back? And the crackers?*

"I hope you don't mind."

I stared at him blankly for a second and said, "Uh, sure. Of course not." This felt like a fairly large red flag had blown across the room and wrapped itself around my head. I recalled in previous conversations that he mentioned how frugal he was. I respected fiscal conservatism, *but WHO TAKES THE CHEESE?*

When I ran this anecdote by some of my clients in our lash-therapy sessions, all kinds of questions came to light, such as: "Was it a special, rare cheese? Was it from Dean and DeLuca or Joan's on Third? Or The Cheese Store of Beverly Hills?"

Maybe there was a chance he thought I wouldn't eat it or maybe he needed it for some reason the next day? But, wouldn't it be just plain good manners to leave it? Just leave the girl some cheese, for crying out loud, so that maybe she would think of you when she took a bite out of it in the middle of the night!

As I walked him to the door that night, I was still busy trying to unwrap the red flag off my head. But my adventures with Cheesy Charlie weren't over yet. He asked me to go to dinner with him after I returned from my camping trip. I told him I'd be back on Sunday and, sure, I'd love to go out for dinner. Even after the cheese incident, I was still willing to see where it would lead. He was cute and kind and fun, and the memories of our amazing first date night were still vivid in my mind. He was also clearly very skilled at making micro salads. *Maybe I'm being too hard on the guy*, I thought.

    I left for my camping trip figuring I would definitely hear from him again. But Thursday passed, then Friday, then Saturday, and I heard nothing from him. Surely, he would have texted at some point. He went right from wanting to get married and wanting to thaw out my eggs … to total silence.

    I sat in the bottom of the Grand Canyon, surrounded by beautiful blue water and ancient stone walls thinking about Charlie. His Havarti-ness had come to haunt me in the Grand Canyon. Oh, the silence and the cheese! *Damn you, Cupid, you are NOT OK!*

    I finally let it go and settled into having a wonderful trip with my family. I wasn't going to let some dairy hoarder ruin my experience in this beautiful place. But, my curiosity was still growing about Cheesy Charlie. What had happened to him? Should I possibly be worried? Was he dead, or just a dick?

    I returned on Sunday and didn't hear from Charlie until Tuesday morning at 8:30 when he sent a text asking if I had been eaten by a bear.

    I responded with, "HI ;) How are you?" Then the line went silent again for twenty-four hours. *Was this normal behavior?* I kind of expected some sort of response from someone who was interested in me. *Was I wrong to expect that?*

    I finally received another random text from him saying, "Not a single picture :(but I get it. Hope you're wonderfully re-engaged with Mother Nature x."

    HMM. Maybe it's an Australian cultural thing? I texted back and asked him if he thought I was still in Mother Nature? Then all of a sudden he texts me, "Welcome back." Now I'm just confused.

The next day I received another text from Charlie that said, "When, oh when, are we kissing again?"

I responded with, "Hi, this weekend, what are you doing?"

Four hours passed, followed by a response of, "Sounds good. Saturday, I'm going to a fortieth birthday party near you."

I responded with, "Cool, what did you have in mind?" THEN TOTAL SILENCE. What did he mean exactly? Was he going to take me to the party? Was he going to stop by before or after for a kiss? I realized I didn't understand men at all anymore. Men and I were speaking two different languages, with no hope of translation.

Forty-eight hours later, on Saturday morning, I received a text from Charlie: "Do you want to come over for lunch?"

I sighed. It was time to cut my losses. All the cheese in the world—or the salmon, or the mini-salads, or the great four-part first dates—was not going to help me understand what made Charlie tick. My desire to be loved and accepted had blindfolded me to the fact that we were not only from two different continents, we were living on two different planets.

I put down my phone. Cupid wasn't going to strike this time. Not with this guy. Clearly, I was going to have to keep looking. It wasn't ideal, but it was okay.

*****

Urban Legend told to me by a man I had one date with:

"So, there's a formula for getting a woman. It's been tried and tested and works without fail. You take a woman to a restaurant. You order her the most gluttonous meal—a pasta dish with heavy cream sauce. She'll feel comfortable around you, let her guard down. Then you take her home and put on some Christmas music. A woman will feel a sense of old times and melancholy, relating back to her childhood.

Then you pull out the champagne and chocolate-covered strawberries and just casually say, 'Hey, why don't we open this?' So now she's feeling special and spontaneous and also trusting. Basically, you have her in the palm of your hand. And you have all the power."

Voilà

The Hungry Hobo

My Zoosk account was lighting up like a California wildfire. I have to admit, Nick's opening message of, "I love you," took me a bit by surprise, but it was a little flattering, and it certainly piqued my curiosity. This guy was ballsy. He told me that, although he had been on Zoosk for less than twenty-four hours and already had a lot of women interested, he would drop them in a heartbeat if I wanted to see him. He wanted to prove his love to me.

I pondered what kinds of things I could ask him to do to prove his love. At this point, my standards were so low, showing up on time and returning phone calls, peppered with the occasional sushi dinner, would qualify as ample proof.

However, I have to admit, I appreciated his putting-it-all-out-there approach. It was a pleasant contrast to the usual male instinct of withholding emotions and information. Plus, he was cute—scruffy hair, smile lines, and an adorable scar on his chin—he had an edgy, Old Hollywood look about him, like if Clark Gable had been slumming around in *Fight Club*.

The messages kept coming. Each one a bit more intriguing. He was born on Cape Cod and grew up in a family of three kids. I instantly related, having grown up going to the Cape once a year since I was six years old. We had an East Coast connection in common, as well as being the baby of the family.

He was creative, which appealed to me. Over text, he spoke of a film he had written, directed, and starred in for under ten grand. I hadn't heard of it, but it won six awards and was featured on the local news. Normally, I try not to date struggling actors or directors, but I liked his openness and emotional availability. I messaged him and asked him where he lived. He gave me his number instead, and I noticed that the first six digits were the same as mine. I took this as a sign that we were geographically simpatico. He told me to give him a call when I had the time and we could arrange to meet.

Intrigued, I called him and suggested that he should drop by my place. He could pick me up and we could take it from there. He said he would stop by later that evening. I was a tiny bit hesitant about having him come over but I felt relatively safe, and I had plenty of protection in my home: bear mace, Bella the cat … What more could one need?

A few hours went by, and I happened to peek out the window right at the moment Nick was coming up the stairs. He had on one of those beanie hats and a lot of prayer beads hanging off his body. He knocked on the door, a little musical knock. Oh boy, I thought, actors!

So, I opened the door and there he stood in the doorway, handsome as hell, with disheveled hair and a River Phoenix vibe. This is a very LA look; you could be a millionaire and still resemble a person who's been living in a tent underneath a bridge somewhere.

His eyes were wide as he stepped inside. He seemed really excited about my place, and he kept saying over and over how great it was. I live in a bungalow in Laurel Canyon with lots of natural light and numerous windows, and I've even got an infrared sauna tucked away neatly near the dining room. It's comfortable in an upscale bohemian kind of way. But, this guy was acting like it was a mansion in the Palisades.

After going on about the furnishings and the kitchen, he turned to me and said, "I know this might sound really odd, but my shower isn't working. Do you mind if I take a quick shower before our date?"

I was confused. Was this how he intended to prove his love? By taking a shower? Then I started thinking about those East Coast similarities. Maybe I shouldn't be so hard on the guy; he was a good guy from a similar family. What was the worst thing that could happen?

"Listen," I said, only half-jokingly, "if you want to give me your wallet and keys, you can take a quick shower." He agreed. The shower started and after a few minutes I could hear the warbling strains of Frank Sinatra's "Luck Be a Lady" coming from the bathroom. The man was easy on the eyes, but he couldn't hit a high note to save his life.

After ten minutes or so of Sinatra, he came out clean and smelling fresh, and looking considerably better than he did when he arrived. Suddenly his whole shower plan seemed like a stroke of genius.

"So, are you hungry?" he asked. "Because I've got a treat for you!"

I smiled, liking the sound of it.

"Actually, I am and I eat pretty much everything. I love exotic random cuisine, anything different," I said.

Clearly, he had planned the beginning of an adventure. The "love-proving" portion of his program was about to begin!

I was curious and excited and knew that wherever we were going, it was probably going to be a little off the beaten path. The way he said the word "treat" had an air of mystery to it, like we were about to pick up a Christmas tree in the middle of July.

We walked out to the street, and I got into his car, a black Volkswagen Golf that had, alas, seen better days. The first thing I noticed as I sat down were all sorts of brightly colored trash flashing at me from the dark abyss of his floorboard—a jigsaw puzzle of crumpled bags from Wendy's, McDonald's, Chick-fil-A, and Carl's Jr. The smell of old French fries rose up all around me like some ungodly perfume.

The thought occurred to me that maybe he had some kind of eating disorder. Maybe, I thought ruefully, that's another thing we have in common? East Coast? Phone digits? Food issues developed by living too many years in the beauty capital of the world?

He fumbled with his keys and then proceeded to jam them in the ignition as he looked over at me. I tried my best to smile through the stale food scent. *Look composed,* I thought. *Don't let on. Just ride it out. Remember, it's an adventure.*

"All right," he said. "Here's the deal. I actually have to work tonight, but I figured we could maybe combine my work with a dinner date?" He smiled at me, pleased.

I was confused. Did he work at Disneyland? How was this going to unfold as an adventure? Did he work at the Magic Castle as a magician? Ooh … this could be fun!

"Excellent!" he said. "One of my survival kind of jobs, when things get a little lean, is that I get paid to rate fast food. Now, I know it seems too good to be true, right? But it's not! Pretty awesome, huh?"

So, wait. Was he saying there was no Magic Castle? He shifted into gear, and I could feel the car start to seize and jerk.

"Sorry, parking brake was on," he said, laughing and rolling his eyes. "Yeah, I go to fast-food drive-thrus. And then I order up whatever and have to rate the whole experience. It's pretty cool, actually. I make money eating and the whole rating thing is kind of like science, you know?" He made a hard right turn and the car went lurching, tires screeching onto Sunset Boulevard.

"I never even knew a job like that existed," I said, utterly baffled.

"Well, welcome to my world. Prepare to exist in the nonexistent." I wasn't sure what that meant. Was that a known slogan? Was he a poet-philosopher of the trans fat set? I gripped the door handle, feeling slightly faint from the residual odor of McNuggets.

Our first stop was Wendy's, followed by Burger King, then In-N-Out Burger. That night we went to not one, not three, not five, but seven different fast-food restaurants! Despite myself, I started to get a feel for the routine of life in "the nonexistent." We would drive up to a place, order a meal, and sit in the parking lot analyzing the whole experience, discussing texture, taste, and the service. There was a form he filled out which rated everything on a scale of one to five, followed by questions that required more detailed, written observations. By the time we got to the last restaurant, lucky number seven, a Del Taco on La Cienega, I had begun to appreciate the difference between the Macho Burrito and the Baconator hamburger.

He had talked about his dreams, aspirations, and his film, and I shared some of my own experiences. We kept the talk pretty light as he finally reclined his seat and sat facing me with his back against the door while he took a bite out of his Baja burrito.

As he took some notes on the quality of the ranchero sauce, I studied him. "So, you've got this movie finished, it's showing at a film festival, and everything seems pretty much on the up and up," I said. "But where do you live? You never told me."

He froze with the burrito still in his mouth.

"Ah jeez, I know, well it's kinda catch as catch can ..." he said nervously.

"Meaning?"

"Well, I mostly ... live in motels and my car."

Wow. That was not what I was expecting.

"What motels? Where do you park your car to sleep in?" I asked.

"I park in grocery store parking lots. And whatever motel is cheap. I try to stay awake at night and nod off during the day."

Nod off during the day? Grocery stores? Is he on Zoosk just so he can find a woman who will let him take a shower? I was torn between deep sadness for this individual and deep discomfort that he might have been using me as the cheapest of all cheap hotel showers.

"Wow. So, like we are basically in your living room right now, huh?"

"Yeah, pretty much," he said with a shrug.

I just shook my head and with a quick smile said, "Look, I have to be honest with you, as you were kind enough to be honest with me, but that's kind of a lot to deal with."

He said, "You know, I totally get it. But, one of these days I'll be on top! You'll be hearing from me then."

"Sounds good," I said. "Well, I probably should head back soon."

"Well, I think we are totally SOULMATES," he said.

Soulmates? Uh oh. I had to nip this in the bud.

"Look, this date has been really interesting," I said. "Truly. It's been *unconventional*. I can tell you're one of those thinking-outside-the-box people and I gotta give you respect for that. Seeing things outside the norm can lead to success."

"Well, thanks for giving a hungry hobo a shot," he said with a smile. "We're all just looking for love, you know?"

He sighed in a curious mixture of both relief and disappointment as he started the car and steered us out of the Del Taco parking lot (their burritos and customer service rated a "5" and a "4" respectively.) We drove back to my place, winding through the canyon streets. He jammed to Def Leppard on the radio. He had an air of the eternal optimist somehow hardwired into his hungry hobo mind, the love child of Pollyanna and Peter Pan.

On the car ride home, all I could think about was rushing upstairs and downing an entire bottle of digestive enzymes. I was fantasizing about having him drop me off at Whole Foods where I could just stand in the aisle guzzling probiotics straight off the shelf. Maybe he could sleep in the parking lot there?

We finally arrived at my house, and I stepped out of the car ending the evening on a high note. "Good luck with everything!" I told him. "It was fun—even though I'm totally sick."

"Thanks!" he said. "It was a blast getting to know you. And like I said, when I'm back on top, you'll be hearing from me!"

I waved and made my way up the stairs. He started to drive off, but then stopped, calling out, "Hey, do you know if it's cool for someone to sleep in their car up here in this neighborhood? Like, do cops roll by a lot?"

I leaned back down to look at him. He sat behind the wheel wearing that same, unflinching Clark Gable smile and goofball glow he had had in his Zoosk profile photo.

"I don't know. Parking lots are probably better."

"Gotcha."

He waved and drove away, taillights finally disappearing. Upward and onward, Hungry Hobo! May the force be with you.

*****

One time I met a man who was very much into saving the tapirs. He had a tattoo of a tapir covering his entire chest. I found it interesting but odd. The trunk of the animal was an extension of another body part for this man. I could just imagine what would happen when he got excited …

Sociopath in the Sauna

"I'M A VERY, VERY BAD MAN."

These words still haunt me and cause me to break out in a sweat, whether I'm in my infrared sauna or not. You see, thanks to this man I now have Sauna Remorse. My infrared sauna, which was once a personal refuge built for relaxation and escape, I now associate with crematoriums and confessional booths.

I met Matthew on Hinge, which was recommended to me by a girlfriend who loved it because it allowed you up to ten matches a day, and it matched you with a mutual friend through Facebook, so you could meet people within one of your social circles—or at least adjacent to one of them.

It hinges on the notion that a friend of a friend is always better than a total stranger. Exactly what was needed to find my future husband! I chose to ignore the fact that by definition, a hinge can get rusty and need constant grease. And it attaches two things together while allowing for limited movement: i.e., no change, no compromise. I ignored the semantics and accepted a match with Matthew, a nice-looking guy who worked in the movie business.

Matthew was a divorced guy in his forties with a recent bit of success. I was hesitant to meet with him at first but my friend Blair kept insisting that I should, so we made plans to meet at Paper or Plastik, an industrial-chic coffeehouse on Pico. When I walked into the café, I noticed him right away. He was tall, legs barely able to fit under the table, wearing dark Ray Bans and an Izod shirt buttoned tightly up to his neck. He was talking on the phone as I approached.

"Well, hello. Glad you could make it," he whispered, smiling. There was a slight gap between his front teeth. I liked it; it weirdly reminded me of Madonna.

"Grab a coffee and put it on my tab," he said, covering the mouthpiece. "I'm just finishing rolling calls, I'll be right with you."

When I came back over with my coffee and settled into the booth next to him his guard seemed to melt. He immediately began asking me questions. The conversation flowed far more easily than it had on any of my last dates. This was great. Hinge, bring me the father of my children!

It turned out Matthew was from England. He'd attended boarding school overseas and then Oxford before making the jump to LA. I was impressed with his education; clearly he was no dummy. He spoke of how hard it was to find true connection even after living here the past twenty years. But I guess he found some connection with me because he wanted to continue the date at a Korean BBQ place called Soot Bull Jeep. I hadn't been there, but it sounded like exactly the things all my other friends were doing on dates with cool, enlightened men. This already seemed very well-oiled.

At Soot Bull Jeep, Matthew did all the ordering. One order of short ribs and one order of the vegetables. "Don't worry. It'll be big enough for the both of us," he said. I sipped my Chung Ha, a Korean-style sake, while he sipped his water. I liked his boyish charm and easygoing personality. He wasn't gorgeous with a capital "G" but there was definitely something interesting about him. After dinner, he asked, "Hey, would you like to come over sometime next week to watch a film I worked on?"

I hesitated for a split second, studying his face, which was open and friendly, Madonna smile on display. "Sure! Sounds great," I said. Why not?

As the following week approached, he thoughtfully texted me throughout the day, asking how work was going or if I had gone to Barry's Bootcamp yet. He showed a genuine curiosity about me and I was happy when he followed through and invited me over the following day to watch his movie.

I arrived on time, moseying up to the front door of a cozy two-bedroom house in the Valley. I had barely walked in the door when he thrust a pair of Bose noise-canceling headphones and his laptop into my hands. He walked me into his bedroom and said, "Now, don't come out until the film's over. I wanna hear your full reaction from start to finish."

I was a little confused. Why weren't we watching it together? Or in a group? Obviously, artists can be sensitive, but this felt extreme, like I had been thrown into some kind of "screening cell." But since I didn't have much of a choice, I sat down on his bed and watched the film. It was exactly ninety-seven minutes long and as soon as the first credit appeared onscreen, he immediately swung the door open to get my reaction. By that time, I was lying fully flat on his very comfortable bed and it's incredibly soft comforter and pillows. Needless to say, my eyes had closed a couple of times. How can a mediocre movie compete with an exceptional bed?

Matthew had an expectant look on his face. "So, what did you think?" he asked, pacing the room with excitement.

"Uhhh …" All I could think about was how tired I was. The idea of having an in-depth discussion in which I would have to deliver a carefully worded film review exhausted me even further. He kept pacing the floor.

"Do you think this could win an Oscar? How was the music? Did I do my job well?

Do you think the critics will like it?"

"You did your job well, yes, and I'm sure people will love it …"

"But, what did you think of the editing?" he said. He continued to interrogate me. I had come here thinking he wanted to share his creativity with me, but now I realized I was just a free test audience. Needless to say, my answers weren't the detailed responses he was hoping for. Each time I failed to give him the response he wanted on the "character arcs" or the "pacing," he would badger me for more details. I bravely attempted to touch on the lighting, the editing, and the performances. I got more enthusiastic as I spoke, finally concluding with, "You know, yeah, I could see it actually getting an award or two if they do all the marketing right ..."

When the word "award" left my lips, his face lit up like one of those clown dolls with the huge eyes that bulge out.

"Really? I think you're right. I can see this being an Oscar picture ..."

He was already beginning to write his speech right then and there.

After that, I wasn't so sure how I felt about Matthew. I knew that I didn't want to talk about his movie again, and that seemed hard to avoid since he was a movie director. But, he kept texting me throughout the next few days, saying kind things and how much he wanted to hang out again. He did not lack persistence.

So, we went out to dinner a few more times, and his movie mercifully only came up here and there. The drinks and the conversation flowed, and we went to interesting restaurants, and a couple of times we met up with some of his friends.

And the attraction between us grew. After a particularly lovely night at Nobu, I shared the most treasured parts of myself with him ... including my infrared sauna.

I came to regret this because after that day, his texts began to always casually mention at the end that he'd "love to pop over and use my sauna." It felt similar to a client texting me asking if she could come in on Friday at four for a lash touch-up. And once I accepted his "appointment," the similarities to my client-lash-artist relationship continued; once he was situated in the sauna with his water bottle, I morphed into his therapist, listening attentively as he spoke about his career anxieties. The only difference was, with a therapist, he probably would have been more honest. But with me, I couldn't help but feel that he was spinning lies here and there. He would say he knew certain people, or mention taking yoga or spin classes ... stuff that didn't add up with previous conversations and timelines.

Gone were the Korean BBQ dinner invitations. Eventually, it got to the point where when he wanted to come over, he would just send a one word text: SAUNA. Truth be told, I didn't mind feeding him, or letting him drink all my Fiji water ... because I still really liked him. In between "SAUNA" requests and alternative-fact-based therapy sessions, I still thought Matthew was a good person. A good person with issues, but still a good person.

But, inevitably, it wore to the point where I began feeling used. Teasingly at first, I suggested that it might be nice if he brought "something" over in exchange for these sauna therapy sessions. He took me up on the idea, texting me that he would bring over a stack of screeners for us to watch. At first I was excited, imagining all the movies I'd been too busy to see in the theater. What would he bring? Hopefully, the new Amy Schumer movie!

But, when he arrived, I saw that his stack of screeners wasn't a cornucopia of movies I'd been dying to see, but rather a fat pile of random television boxed sets marked "For Your Emmy Consideration." They were TV episodes that anyone with a Netflix subscription could watch anytime they wanted.

On another occasion, after a "SAUNA" text, he added, "I'm bringing you dinner!" When he arrived, I learned that dinner was leftover food from the African restaurant he dined at earlier that day with his son. As I glumly ate my half box of bobotie, I couldn't help feeling that Matthew was a sauna vampire, sucking infrared rays and free therapy from me as I continued to foolishly hope for a real connection. No amount of leftover food or Netflix screeners could provide the kind of transfusion I needed to wake up and see the light.

But still I held onto a shred of hope, like any good vampire-addict does. When the next "SAUNA" text popped up on my phone, I asked him what he was bringing. "You're gonna love it," he said. An hour later he arrived with a bag of t-shirts, all of them extra small and tight, that had been worn by a group of dancers from a hip-hop music video shoot. Not only were they not something I would ever wear, they also had the extra fun of making me feel fat.

I took a few deep breaths and tried to let go of my insecurities, because soon we would be sitting in the red glow of the sauna, the heat rising around us, and all our troubles would melt away …

As the sweat began to pour from our pores, he looked at me carefully with a mint-flavored toothpick hanging from his lips like a warped cigarette.

"I need to confess something," he said.

"Sure," I said, even though I was already feeling quite overheated.

"I'm a very, very bad man," he said.

Wait. What?

The temperature started to rise. Where was this going?

"I've slept with over one thousand women. Sometimes three in a single day," he confessed.

"Whoa! That's a big number," I said, trying to add this all up in my mind. Who sleeps with three people in a day?!?

"So … you're a sex addict?" I said.

"Maybe? I think I've gotten it under control, though. I'm trying to get back together with my girlfriend. It would be good to have real support for a change. Settle down," he said. He let the toothpick hang in his mouth.

"Girlfriend? You never mentioned a … girlfriend," I said. I wasn't expecting that.

"I ghost a lot of women. Like, right now I'm seeing three women at once, but I feel like I need to change my ways."

"Ghosting? What is that?" I asked.

"It's like pretending people don't exist. Disappearing. Not responding."

Suddenly his random absences were making sense. He wiped sweat off his face, frustrated. "I don't know. I gotta get out of this town! I feel like Hollywood is destroying me! I've been having sex with girls that think they're gonna get parts. It's such a cliché. I've practically got a fucking casting couch in my living room. It just DOESN'T STOP!"

He took a long sip of the complimentary Fiji water. I remained motionless, trying to process this, as we sat in the hot silence for a long time. "Sometimes, I think I don't really have any feelings or emotions," he said, staring at the red light in the sauna. "I think … I might be a sociopath."

Shortly after that, I asked him to leave. After he'd gone and after I'd vigorously scrubbed his sociopathic sweat from my personal refuge, I realized in an odd way I felt some respect for him, having come clean about his bad behavior. It was interesting to have someone who holds themselves in such high regard divulge their most shameful secrets to you.

I had been drawn into Matthew's charms, largely because of the positive qualities he possessed, and also because I wanted very much to believe that this was the type of responsible, successful man I could be in love with and who would love me back. It just took me a while to see that; while he may have been a few of those things, he was more notably a sex addict with low self-esteem who could love only himself.

I still receive the random text from Matthew, like a knock on my door checking to see if maybe my resistance is down for a second. But I've stopped responding. I've finally learned that with certain people, you have to cut and run. With certain people, you just have to ghost.

*****

A guy picks me up in an orange Hummer.
We go on a sushi date.
He explains that he is getting out of real estate to pursue acting.
He said he just got Botox.
"How does my face look? Do I have any wrinkles?"

The Groupon Gigolo

"Oh, I'd know that sound anywhere. You drive a BMW, don't you?"

"Ummm, yeah," I said as I turned on the ignition.

That was my first phone introduction to Tommy. He was introduced to me by a client who said we would be perfect together. Seemingly so, our phone conversation was comfortable and easy. A music producer by trade, Tommy was calling from a radio station with one of the bands he produced, and they were doing an on-air interview. His interest in the arts was inspiring; finally someone who could help keep me apprised on the latest releases. We ended our conversation and decided to meet for sushi at this cozy little spot on La Cienega. According to Tommy, the fish had been flown in that day and apparently, the toro was "mouthwatering."

Not only was Tommy up on music, but he was clearly up on raw fish, as well. This Tommy was sounding more awesome by the minute. As I proceeded to get ready, I found myself getting excited. Tommy had been easy, and I hadn't felt that ease in quite some time. To calm my optimistic nerves, I had a glass of wine and smoked a hidden cigarette. After I sprayed some Serge Lutens Fleurs d'Oranger to mask the smell of smoke, I took a swig of mouthwash and was out the door.

Tommy had asked to pick me up, and based on our conversations about BMWs, I was expecting him to be driving one. But there he was, standing with the passenger side door open to a large black 2016 sedan.

He looked to be in his early fifties, stood about five foot six with lifts on, and was wearing all black with a biker jacket. His salt-and-pepper hair was styled into a Fonzie type of do with enough grease to fry a corn dog. He gave me a kiss on my cheek, which was so forceful and hard it actually hurt. His scent of Yves Saint Laurent Kouros cologne was so strong it overpowered my scent.

He settled me into my seat, then made his way to the driver's side. He asked, "Do you smoke?"

"No, not normally. But a friend left a random cigarette at my house and I had a couple drags a few hours ago. Can you smell it?"

"Yeah, I can," he said. I felt like an idiot. Why did I do that? Everyone knows as much and as hard as you try to mask the smell of cigarette smoke, it stays soaked on you like an old tattoo. Tommy just shrugged it off and said, "No biggie." But I could tell he was annoyed. He must have been if he brought it up, right?

"So, what kind of car is this?" I asked, genuinely curious. Tommy nodded, as he started the engine and we drove down Laurel Canyon. "It's a Cadillac. I work for Capitol Records and they give me an allowance for a car. Most people who work there get Caddies."

"That's awesome," I said. "You're so lucky!" He went on about how he wanted a BMW, but he's going to take the extra allowance next year to get one and pay extra.

"Why would you do that?" I asked him. "When you have free transportation?"

He shrugged. "I'm more of a BMW-type of guy." By the way he drove, I could tell he thought he was an awesome driver, hugging the curves and gunning it to pass cars. He wasn't a yuppie but had an air of snobbery attached.

I started to notice that so much of Tommy's existence was about appearance. He wanted to fully play the part of "cool music producer with an edge," which confused me because wasn't it enough that he was a cool music producer with an edge? If he was, why did he have to try so hard to play one?

Throughout dinner, he talked about the bands he had managed and how much money he'd made on them. He spoke of his travels to Bali and how he used to surf but no longer had time for it. He spoke of his divorce seven years prior. How his ex had left him for another woman. How she and her wife got married last year, and he wasn't invited to the wedding. I started to sense how insecure Tommy was. Clearly, he was still trying to prove himself at age fifty. I had compassion and an appreciation for him though, because underneath it all, he simply wanted to be seen and accepted, especially after a painful divorce. I enjoyed sake throughout the dinner and noticed he hardly had any. He mentioned that he didn't really drink much anymore and instead partakes in medical weed. He said how much better marijuana is compared to alcohol, and that there are fewer mishaps when it comes to stoners as opposed to alcoholics.

The check arrived, and I excused myself to the bathroom to avoid any awkwardness. When I returned I noticed a piece of folded-over paper on the bill holder. "What's that?" I asked.

"Oh, gosh," he said. "Have you ever been on Groupon?"

Oh, no. Did this guy actually use a Groupon to pay for dinner? Yep, he did. Tommy went on to say how you can find great deals on Groupon and it's fun, too, because it encourages you to try new places. I was speechless realizing that this whole spiel about the freshest fish and the most mouthwatering toro had been ripped straight from the Groupon description.

On the drive home, Tommy went on about how much he enjoyed the sushi and would love to hang out again. I just nodded my head and when we got to my house, quickly gave him a peck on the cheek and thanked him for a lovely evening.

A couple of days went by, and I received a text from Tommy asking how I was doing. It was a nice gesture to check in. He asked if I wanted to go drive some race cars on the track in Corona. I thought, *Wow, that sounds like a fun, out of the ordinary experience.* I said, yes.

Tommy suggested we meet at his apartment and we'd make our way to Corona. Driving race cars was definitely a unique experience. *Maybe Tommy's "record producer with an edge" act was more real than I had initially thought.*

I meet him at his apartment the following day. But before I set foot inside, he asked me to take off my shoes. His housekeeper had just been there, he said, and he wanted to keep his apartment as clean as possible. I noticed that in his kitchen he had an assortment of bongs, gummy worms, goldfish, and lemonade all spread out on his table. He pointed to them and laughed, saying his housekeeper probably may have some cause for concern. Turns out they were all marijuana edibles.

I looked around his place, which I had to admit was beautiful in a modern way, with nice furniture and décor. There were Fred Segal bags full of clothing, and his bedroom contained a yellow SoulCycle bike. This guy clearly liked the finer things. And he liked them very, very organized. Everything was squeaky clean to an extreme. I understood why he had all those weed gummy worms; the guy needed to relax.

We made our way down to the garage and he instructed me to give him my keys. Did he want to move my car to a better parking space? No, he said, he wanted to drive my car. "Let me be your chauffer for the day," he said.

So we began our drive out to Corona. For some reason, the day already had a dull air about it. Tommy started to talk about himself again and his relationships. He kept saying how comfortable he felt with me and how easy I was to talk to. It took no effort, he said, and he felt like he could tell me anything. But he wanted to make sure that I knew that he could only offer dinner and sex, nothing more serious. *Wow, did that really come out of his mouth?*

"That's fine," I said. "No worries."

He went on about how he fell out of love with his ex and how he wanted to be a free spirit. I couldn't help but think: *This guy has so many conflicting characteristics: he wants to be a free spirit, but he is also deeply controlling; he's cheap, but he has expensive tastes; he wants to be "edgy," but he's really just anal.*

We finally made it to the racetrack, which was a welcome change of scenery after the car ride. Having an adrenaline rush would be a welcome relief. We got our cars and raced around the track at 140 mph. I felt fantastic. The old energy from the car ride was being whisked away. We whizzed around the track for over two hours. Sometimes we would drive together and then other times we would just watch the other cars as they sped by. I was glad I had given Tommy another chance. Everyone has things to work on, and I was beginning to think Tommy was a diamond in the rough. After laughing and driving and thoroughly enjoying ourselves, our session was up, and we made our way to the cashier. Once we got there, Tommy reached for his back wallet—and pulled out a folded piece of white paper.

I stared at the paper. This couldn't be … another Groupon, could it?

Everything seemed like it was going in slow motion. The unfolding of the paper, the handing it over to the cashier. A sushi-dinner Groupon was one thing, but a race-car-driving experience Groupon? My mind flashed forward to ten years from now with Tommy and our life living on Groupons. I could see him pulling out Groupons for teeth whitening, Botox, bad folk concerts, Lasik surgery, couples therapy …

I was silent on the way home and allowed him to talk more about the things and activities he wanted to do with me. But I couldn't stop imagining that our vacations would be be a ten-day Peru tour with airfare, car, and hotel for $1,599. Would my wedding be paid for with Groupons? I understand and respect fiscal conservatism. But for every single experience?

We made it back to Hollywood. Tommy asked if I wanted to grab some dinner. There was a new ramen place he'd been wanting to try. Undoubtedly, thanks to another folded piece of paper in his wallet.

"Today was a beautiful day with you," I said. "But I just think you and I are better off being friends. We want different things. You want dinner and sex and I want something else."

XO

*****

On dating sites, men state that they are always taller than they actually are. If they are five feet five inches tall, then shouldn't they simply state they are five feet five inches tall? Do they think that I will like them more when I realize they are six inches shorter in real life?

Portland Pete

I was trying the dating site Match for the first time and, as is par for the course, became fascinated by the word itself. I thought about match tips bursting into flames with the possibility of love, followed by strong signals of WARNING. FIRE. DANGER. As much as the romantic in me didn't want to admit it, the cynic in me cautioned that playing with matches rarely ends well.

Through Match, I received an email from a guy in Portland, Oregon, named Pete who owned an advertising agency. Pete was forty-one and spent four months out of the year surfing on the North Shore of Oahu. My interest was piqued. In his two photos on Match, one was of him at a bar with a group of friends and the other was a photo of him hiking alone. I was a little concerned because neither picture was totally in focus. He seemed attractive, yet he was wearing sunglasses, so I only got a vague sense of what he looked like. But he had a friendly, charming smile that distinguished itself in the blur.

His email message to me was an unusual pitch. He explained that he wasn't really a dating-site type of guy, and that he was only on Match for a day because the staff of the firm he owned had signed him up. They wanted to choose a girl they thought would be right for him, and apparently they chose me. Pete said I was their first choice. I was flattered, and also I found it endearing that his employees would care so much about him that they wanted him to find his true love ... aka me?

He said that he wanted to fly me to Portland first class and put me up in a five-star hotel for the weekend. A free trip to a place I'd never been before with a cute guy who had been hand-chosen by a staff of fairy-god employees? Sign me up! Of course, he could also be a total loon who crept around on dating sites looking for foolish, unsuspecting women to bring

109

to his isolated cabin in the wilderness. How could I tell if he was dragging me to a five-star hotel of backwoods insanity?

My inner romantic reminded my inner cynic that we were on Match to take a chance and possibly light the fire of love, so I called him up. We had a great conversation, ranging from his being a victim of credit card fraud to his surf adventures. Finally, I voiced some of my concern.

"How do I know that you're not totally crazy and you're not going to throw me in the trunk of your car?" I asked him, half joking.

"Well, I have a hard enough time just approaching a woman, much less throwing one in the trunk of my car!" Pete responded, laughing. "There's a reason the people at my office put me on Match, you know? You're more than welcome to talk to any of them."

His self-effacing vibe and good personality made me feel better about the idea of meeting him. But before I committed fully to planning the trip, on a whim, I suggested that we have a three-way call with my dad. After all, a guy could lie to a girl on the phone, but would he really have the gall to lie to her dad? Plus, my dad is an excellent judge of character. Whenever my dad disapproves of something he would give an explanation—usually via letter—as to why my life would be ruined if I didn't take his advice, followed by a long list of excellent points. One time, he talked me out of dating someone who was over $200,000 in debt and also had anger issues. The other time it was a letter forbidding me to pose in *Playboy*. Go figure!

Fortunately, Pete agreed to speak to my dad without hesitation. Our three-way phone call was easy, light, and fun. I could picture Pete and my parents and I sitting around the table at Christmas, hanging stockings, singing carols … Okay, so maybe I was taking it too far, but, hey, at least now my parents had all of Pete's information. I was going to Oregon. The match had been struck!

I was all packed and heading to the airport a week later when I started second-guessing everything. Was I out of my mind? This was crazy, wasn't it?

I calmed myself down, got settled into my first-class seat on Alaskan Airlines, and decided to just leave it in God's hands. There was no turning back at that point.

Promptly after the seat-belt sign went off, it seemed like a good time to order a Bloody Mary. Or perhaps to quell my nerves, a double Bloody Mary was in order. I told myself anxiety was totally normal given the situation. I kept repeating in my head over and over again that I should remain calm and open.

When I finally stumbled into Portland International, I saw some texts from Pete that appeared strangely possessive.

His first text was: "Where are you?"

Second text: "What are you doing? Are you here already?"

Third text: "Do u want me to pick u up?"

No, I did not want him to pick me up. I needed time to go to the hotel and brush my teeth and hair. I hadn't even met this guy and already I needed space!

I texted him back telling him I didn't need a ride, and that I was fine, and that I wouldn't want to pull him away from work. He said, of course, I was probably tired from the flight. We arranged to meet later that evening at the hotel bar before heading out to a new restaurant that he was sure I'd love.

I caught a cab to the Kimpton River Place Hotel. It was really beautifully situated, right on the Willamette River, encompassed by Mother Nature. I managed to check in without any problems. I took the elevator to my room where I was greeted with a gigantic basket with champagne and chocolate-covered cherries sitting on top of a king-sized bed. What a thoughtful gesture, I said to myself. I looked around the room to see a beautiful suite with French doors and a view that looked onto the streets of downtown Portland. I was touched that here was a guy that did what he said he was going to do.

I had a few hours to kill before getting ready to go downstairs, so I moved the basket of cherries and champagne to the table and stretched out on the bed. I sank into the goose down comforter and set the alarm on my phone. It was like pure heaven to lie down. Soon, I was sound asleep, the anxiety from the previous hours a distant memory. When I woke up, two hours later, my anxiety was back in full bore. But I took a shower, got dressed, and made my way downstairs.

At the entrance of the bar I was greeted by an acne-prone hostess. I explained to her that I was looking for someone by the name of Pete. I asked if he had arrived, but he hadn't, so I sat down at a small table in the corner by a large window where I could see the rain-soaked streets outside. The weather had been dreary when I arrived, but the rain had really started coming down after I'd woken up from my nap. I looked out the window and stared at the reflection of the streetlights shining on the wet sidewalk. The nervousness began creeping up on me again. I wanted something to drink but there wasn't a server in sight, and I didn't feel like walking over to the bar and fighting my way through the drunken group of young professionals who had dominated the entire restaurant.

Now I had been waiting close to fifteen minutes and was getting slightly annoyed. That's when I saw this man across the room. He was walking at an extremely fast pace straight toward me. *Is that him? He said he was five foot eleven. No way that's him. That guy is five foot five, tops.* I looked down to my phone to see if he had texted since he was running late. I thought about texting him: HEY! WHERE ARE YOU? ARE YOU HERE ALREADY??? DO YOU NEED ME TO COME PICK YOU UP? I looked up from my phone and there he was.

"Hey, I'm Pete," he said.

Holy shit!

"Wow! You are so much more beautiful in person," he said.

I began to see why his photos had been so blurry. He wasn't totally unattractive, except for the lying about his height (and it's the *lying*, not the height, that was unattractive), but he had the smallest eyes that I'd ever seen before. It was like he had the points of a pencil in place of where his eyes should have been.

Oh my goodness! The huge wraparound sunglasses! That's why he was wearing those! But, I wasn't going to judge a man by the size of his eyes.

"It's really nice to meet you," I said, smiling at him as he sat down. "Thank you so much for all of this. The flight and the hotel, all of it has just been fantastic."

"Oh, no problem! It's really my pleasure. I don't get too many gorgeous blondes from LA coming up to see me very often. In fact, you would be the only one," he said. He smiled. It almost completely erased the pencil points in his eyes. He sat down at the table and a waitress practically materialized out of nowhere. *Where the heck had she been all night?*

"Two shots of Gran Patron Platinum Silver Tequila!" he suddenly blurted out while slapping his hands down on the table.

Wow. Okay. I like a man who takes the initiative to order. He had really demanded those tequila shots. It had even startled the waitress. She came back quickly with the shots, and as soon as they were on the table he grabbed both of them and knocked them back. It had happened so fast. I was confused. The two shots were both for him?

"Man! Now that's tequila!" he said, wiping his mouth with his hand.

"I thought one of those was for me," I told him.

"Oh! Well, you didn't have a drink in front of you. I just assumed you didn't want anything," he said.

"Well, I could've definitely used one. But, no worries."

"Well, let's go," he said briskly. "I want to take you to this restaurant. You can have a drink there! My Range Rover is parked right outside and I want you to listen to some music. I've got some friends who are deep into the underground rock scene here, and they just released a new record. It's called *Power Plant People*."

We walked out to his car and he didn't bother to open the door for me, of which I didn't judge him for given the tequila situation in the bar. The inside of his Range Rover smelled strongly of Nag Champa, however. I thought this was a bit odd, given his preppy Izod gingham long-sleeved shirt and his penny loafers.

"Here. Check this out! These are my friends," he said putting a disc into the CD player. I started to feel trapped. Portland Pete had taken the reins, and he seemed to have no interest in anything I had to say. He hadn't even asked how I was doing. He was very different from the person I had spoken with on the phone. He wasn't the psychopath that I'd worried he would be, he was just totally self-absorbed. "The name of their band is Kracker Jack Hi-Way. How cool is that?" he said.

"That's fascinating," I told him. "Sounds really deep."

"Yeah, these guys are so underground that they're not even signed. In fact, they don't even believe in getting signed. They're all about the art, you know?" He hit play and the music that came out of the speakers sounded like pure industrial sludge; the sound of techno drums, greasy guitars and hammers being beaten against sheet metal while a female voice screamed, "I DON'T WANT TO PANIC IN FOREVER."

I didn't want to panic in forever either, so I made the bold move of turning the volume down. "So, tell me about Portland? Do you like living here?" I asked.

"It's pretty cool. It's chill. But, I bet it's probably not as cool as living in LA." Now, I wished I hadn't turned the music down. He seemed to ache with a desperate desire to appear cool, hip, and youthful. The rest of our conversation in the car ride and throughout dinner was about LA and how cool it must be to live there. But, despite his interest in the City of Angels, he never once asked me about my life there. It turned out that he had been to LA a few times on business, but the only thing he seemed determined to do was talk about himself and his past moments of glory south of the Oregon border.

Where was the guy I talked to on the phone? And where, most importantly, was my drink going to come from, and how quickly could it be immediately injected into my bloodstream?

Once we were seated at the restaurant, the whole date began to fragment like a satellite that had fallen from space and was burning apart as it hurled into the atmosphere. I gave up trying to hold a normal conversation and began to order a steady round of gin and tonics to create a barrier against the unending self-absorption coming from the other side of the table.

"Yeah, the last time I was in LA—"

"Let me guess, you ran into Benicio Del Toro eating a Monte Cristo at Canter's Deli?" I said, interrupting him. At this point I was just trying to have a little fun.

"No, I was at this—"

"Kundalini yoga retreat for pregnant teens?" I said.

"It was this restaurant on Sunset and my client had forgotten his wallet!" he said. He hadn't even heard me.

Dinner finally ended and he drove me back to the hotel with the caterwauling sounds of Kracker Jack Hi-Way playing softly in the background. When we pulled up, I gave him a quick hug. I moved fast because I didn't want him getting any ideas about coming up to the room.

"Well, I have to work in the morning, but I have a massage booked for you at eleven o'clock," he called after me as I leapt out of the Range Rover. "We can touch base in the morning and take it from there!"

"Okay, that sounds nice. I'll just talk to you in the morning. Be safe," I said. I watched him pull away from the hotel. I felt a huge wave of relief as he drove away. The date was over, but I felt a little uneasy about the massage. I'd already been fantasizing about catching a flight out early the next morning. I just didn't think I could get through another night of Portland Pete.

I woke up at nine o'clock that morning, still unsure exactly what I was going to do. The massage was a nice gesture, but if I was going to catch a plane, I'd need to check out by noon. Ten o'clock rolled around, and I found myself staring out the window at the bleak weather and wet streets below. The rain never seemed to stop here. I closed my eyes for a second and the images in my head were of huge power plants, endless rows of them being drenched by massive sheets of rain.

It was ten-thirty, and I still hadn't heard from Pete. Out of curiosity, I decided to call down to the spa in the hotel and see how long the massage actually was. When I inquired about my appointment, the girl informed that there was no such appointment on the books. Huh, that's odd. Pete lacked certain qualities, but he'd always been a man of his word, hadn't he?

I texted him and sent a friendly message asking him what was going on. At eleven thirty he finally responded, "Sorry. I thought I'd booked the massage. I'll make it up to you, and we'll go see my friend's band play tonight at a warehouse by the river."

At the mention of the word "band," I had already started packing. By the time "warehouse" came out, I'd tossed everything in the bag. At "river," my suitcase was zipped. I checked out of the hotel at exactly ten minutes till twelve.

While I was waiting for a cab outside, I sent Pete a final text, "Thanks so much for everything, but I've got to catch a flight back home today. The chemistry just isn't there. Hope you understand. Give my best to the band tonight."

When I got to the airport, I walked up to the Alaskan Airlines counter and asked when the next flight out to Los Angeles would be. "I'll take anything," I said, "I'd take a seat on a cargo plane at this point. I just need to get back home. *Immediately.*"

I must have had a look of desperation on my face because the guy behind the ticket counter smiled very calmly and said, "It's going to be okay. I have an economy seat available for the three o'clock flight to LA this afternoon." He winked and said, "Too much rain up here, huh?"

I handed him my credit card. "Something like that," I told him. I smiled for the first time all day.

On the flight home, I thought about the whole experience. Flying somewhere to meet a total stranger in another city is probably something I will never do again. But, it had been an instructive and interesting trip. It had its moments of fun even if the primary one was being totally unconscious in a beautiful king-sized bed with the incredibly soft pillows. Evidently, I had flown all the way to Oregon just to get a terrific night's sleep.

Portland Pete never responded to my final text. I wondered what he would end up telling the people in his office. Would they worry that he would never find love? Would he? Would I? Would we all? I told myself not to worry; these were anxieties to ponder at a later date. Right now, thanks to Alaska Airlines, I was riding that big Kracker Jack Hi-Way in the sky, on my way back home to the Land of the Sun.

*****

Potential Mate: Awww. I was really liking you. I wish you would have read my profile. I really think we could have had something.

Me: **YOU ARE MARRIED**

Potential Mate: I know. Doesn't mean my emotions are so small that love has to be limited.

Dating Detox

Through these experiences and mostly, let's admit it—failed matches, I still haven't found love. But I have gained a whole heck of a lot of insight.

I've learned that I'm not ever going to win on Music Jeopardy. I learned that I probably should have been born in another country, and if there happens to be a music trivia night, I'm better off watching *Grease* on Netflix. I learned not to fly out to meet dates who wear sunglasses in photos. I realized it's wise to be cautious of those who make you food and then take it back home. I learned all about ghosting, and that it's a good policy to practice kindness and gentleness to your dates, since you never know what kind of hard time they're going through. I've learned that growing older isn't necessarily a bad thing.

But most of all, I learned what I want going forward in life. There have been times when I've desperately wondered: "How did I get myself in yet another crazy situation?!" Then I realized the answer was simple. There was a lesson that still needed to be learned. And no matter how many disastrous dates it takes, I'm never going to stop falling in love with learning the lessons in my life.

Until then, love is in formaldehyde ... or so it seems.

ACKNOWLEDGMENTS

My thanks to the beautiful people who made this book possible.

Chance G. Tomlin, who spent endless hours with me writing, editing and making me a better writer. I love your humor and patience.

Kirsten Smith, aka Kiwi, for encouraging me to keep going, being a mentor, having faith in me, and adding sparkle to my work. I am grateful for your friendship.

My mom and dad, who have always been there and have seen my potential. I love you.

Sheri, for your friendship, faith in me, and guidance.

Kurt Lustgarten, for helping with the design.

Blair at authentik creative, inc., for the graphic design, your laughter and all the encouragement. You are special.

Juliette Lewis, who made me believe these stories needed to be told.

Kristin Chenoweth for your support, love and friendship.

My wonderful clients, who have supported me and have been so generous in sharing their stories.

And lastly, to the men who inspired and helped inform these essays …

God Bless!

www.ingramcontent.com/pod-product-compliance
Lightning Source LLC
LaVergne TN
LVHW051501070426
835507LV00022B/2873